A New True Book

THE GREENHOUSE EFFECT

By Darlene R. Stille

CP CHILDRENS PRESS®
CHICAGO

The huge Lincoln Park Conservatory greenhouse in Chicago contains hundreds of plant specimens.

PHOTO CREDITS

AP/Wide World Photos—30 (right), 32 (left)

© Cameramann International, Ltd.—6 (bottom left), 25 (left), 40, 44 (top)

© Joan Dunlop—20 (center right)

© Virginia Grimes—32 (right)

H. Armstrong Roberts—18, 20 (left); © J. Irwin, 23 (top); © W. Pote, 24; © R. J. Bennet, 30 (left)

© Jerry Hennen—20 (bottom right), 38 (left & top right)

Journalism Services—© Joe Jacobson, 12, 14; © Mike Kidulich, 23 (bottom left); © Tim McCabe, 28; © Dave Brown, 34 (left); © Ingrid Johnsson—34 (right), 35 (right)

© Mary Messenger—36 (2 photos)

© Norma Morrison—8, 20 (top right), 31 (right), 44 (bottom right)

Odyssey Productions—© Robert Frerck, 2, 17 (right), 37 (left), 41 (left), 44 (bottom left)

© Rob Outlaw—17 (top left)

Photri—6 (top), 19, 25 (right), 26

Root Resources—45 (right); © Mary M. Tremaine, 31 (left)

© James P. Rowan, 6 (bottom right)

Shostal Associates/SuperStock International, Inc.: © Ernest Manewal, 37 (right)

Tom Stack & Associates—© Ann Duncan, 35 (left); © W. Perry Conway, 41 (right); © F. Stuart Westmoreland, 42 (left); © Gary Milburn, 42 (right); © Thomas Kitchin, 43 (bottom right); © Jack Swenson, 43 (top right); © Robert Winslow, 45 (left)

© Lynn Stone—4

SuperStock International, Inc.—© Robert Llewellyn, Cover

Valan—© Harold V. Green, 17 (bottom left); © Richard T. Nowitz, 23 (bottom right); © V. Wilkinson, 27; © Pierre Kohler, 38 (bottom right); © Thomas Kitchin, 43 (left)

Diagram by Chuck Hills—11

Cover—Sunlight through ferns

Library of Congress Cataloging-in-Publication Data

Stille, Darlene R.
  The greenhouse effect / by Darlene R. Stille.
    p.   cm. — (A New true book)
  Includes index.
  Summary: Describes the causes and effects of the greenhouse effect and how it might be stopped.
  IBSN 0-516-01106-5
  1. Greenhouse effect, Atmospheric—Juvenile literature. [1. Greenhouse effect, Atmospheric. 2. Global warming.] I. Title.
QC912.3.S75 1990   90-2147
363.73'87—dc20   CIP
                                               AC

TABLE OF CONTENTS

THE GREENHOUSE EFFECT AND THE WEATHER

The world may be growing warmer. The Earth's climate may be changing. This is because of something scientists call the "greenhouse effect." It could change the weather all over the world.

To understand the greenhouse effect, we must learn about greenhouses and how they work.

Greenhouses may be large or small,
but they all feature glass or clear
plastic walls and roofs that trap
heat from the Sun's rays inside.

HOW A GREENHOUSE WORKS

A greenhouse is a building made especially for plants. In a greenhouse, flowers can grow when it is snowing outside. Vegetables can grow when the temperature outside is below freezing.

In a greenhouse the walls and roof are made of glass or clear plastic. The Sun's rays warm the air, the soil, and everything else inside the greenhouse.

The light and warm air in a greenhouse let plants grow, even in winter.

But the heat made inside by the Sun's rays cannot escape very easily. The heat is trapped. A greenhouse is also called a hothouse because the air inside gets so warm.

PLANET EARTH'S GREENHOUSE

The Earth we live on is a planet orbiting the Sun in space. Space is empty and cold. The heat made by the Sun's rays on Earth's surface would escape into space if there wasn't something there to stop it. If our planet was not wrapped in its own "greenhouse," nothing could live on Earth.

9

Earth's greenhouse is made of gases.

The gases are clear and invisible. Yet they work just like the glass of a greenhouse.

Rays of sunlight shine through the gases around Earth. This heats Earth's surface. Some of the heat is trapped by certain gases.

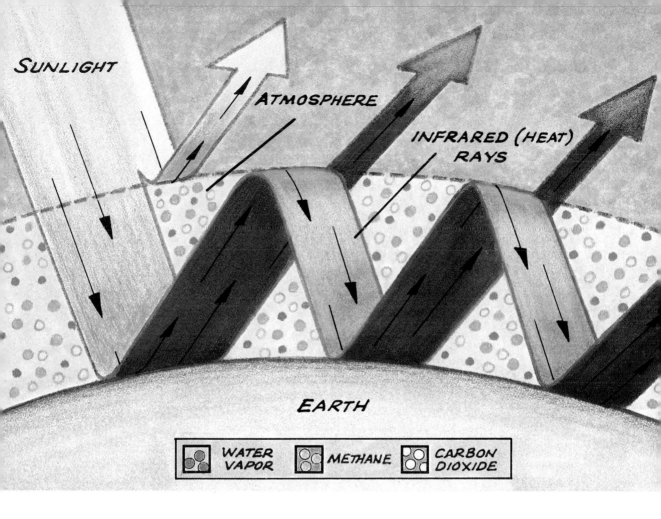

SUNLIGHT

ATMOSPHERE

INFRARED (HEAT) RAYS

EARTH

WATER VAPOR   METHANE   CARBON DIOXIDE

The Sun's rays are changed to heat when they strike Earth's surface. Extra heat passes out into space unless it is blocked by gases in the atmosphere.

This is called the *natural* greenhouse effect. It keeps the Earth warm enough for plants to grow and for animals to live.

GAS AS GLASS

How can gas act like glass? They seem to be so very different.

Glass is solid. It feels hard when we touch it. We cannot squeeze it.

But gas is not solid. We can even put our hand through gas. Try to grab a handful of air. Air is gas. You cannot feel it when you squeeze air. You cannot see it all around you.

Yet glass and gas have something in common. They are both made of *molecules*. Molecules are tiny bits of matter much too small for us to see.

The tightly packed molecules in a glass tumbler can hold water and even solid objects like this pencil.

In glass, the molecules are packed tightly together. This makes glass solid. In a gas, the molecules are very far apart.

But gas molecules, just like glass molecules, can block heat rays trying to escape from Earth's surface.

NATURAL
GREENHOUSE GASES

There are many kinds of gases in nature. Some are better at trapping heat than others.

Earth's natural greenhouse gases include water vapor, carbon dioxide, and methane. These gases are in Earth's atmosphere, the air above the surface of Earth.

Carbon dioxide is Earth's main greenhouse gas. It flows in a cycle.

Carbon dioxide is taken out of the air by green plants. It also gets dissolved in the ocean.

When the plants die or are eaten, carbon dioxide is returned to the air. Animals breathe it out, too.

This cycle—from plants to animals and back to plants— keeps the right balance of

Green plants (top left) take up carbon dioxide from the air. When plants decay (bottom left) the carbon dioxide is released into the air. Animals breathe out carbon dioxide.

carbon dioxide in Earth's atmosphere. If there were too little carbon dioxide, Earth would be too cold for living things. If there were too much, Earth would be too hot.

17

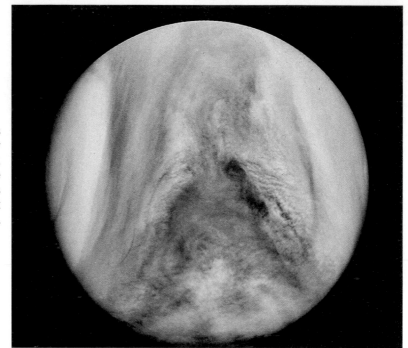

Venus is
covered by
a thick
atmosphere
that is
98 percent
carbon dioxide.

Spacecraft visiting other planets have discovered what too much of these greenhouse gases will do. The planet Venus has an atmosphere that is thick with carbon dioxide. The average temperature on Venus is about 850° F. Venus is too hot for living things.

The planet Neptune has no greenhouse gases in its atmosphere. The temperature on Neptune is about -360° F. Neptune is too cold for living things.

The planet Neptune, photographed by the spacecraft *Voyager II*

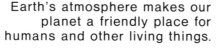

Earth's atmosphere makes our planet a friendly place for humans and other living things.

Earth is the only known planet on which there are living things. The greenhouse gases in Earth's atmosphere give Earth a climate that

is perfect for supporting life.

HOW EARTH MIGHT GROW HOTTER

Earth could grow hotter if more greenhouse gases go up into the atmosphere. This will lead to an increase in the Earth's natural greenhouse effect.

The natural greenhouse effect results from gases that occur in the atmosphere naturally.

The increase in the greenhouse effect is caused by gases sent into the atmosphere by human activities. The cars people drive give off carbon dioxide in their exhaust. Smoke from coal-burning factories and electric power plants sends large amounts of carbon dioxide into the atmosphere.

Smoke from factory chimneys and exhaust from cars contain carbon dioxide that increases the greenhouse gases in the atmosphere.

Plants (left) decay underwater in flooded rice paddies, giving off carbon dioxide. Smoke containing carbon dioxide (above) rises from a coal mine in Virginia.

Farming puts methane into the atmosphere. Decaying plants in rice paddies give off methane. Cows and other farm animals give off methane. Methane also comes from coal mines.

Manufactured gases called CFCs are also increasing the greenhouse effect. CFCs come from air conditioners, refrigerators, plastic foam containers, and some spray cans. CFCs are very powerful blockers of escaping heat rays.

Some spray cans contain harmful gases. This label shows the can contains 40 percent fluorinated hydrocarbons.

or effect of use, seller makes no warranty, express or implied, nor accepts responsibility whether or not used in accordance with directions.

Baby Blue, No. 1902

Pigment		4.13%
Titanium Dioxide	98.70%	
Iron Blue	0.87%	
Phthalocyanine Green	0.43%	
Non-volatile (from vehicle)		11.77%
Cellulose Nitrate, Oil Free Alcohol Derived Alkyd, Coconut Oil Modified Alkyd, Dioctyl Phthalate		
Volatile		44.10%
Ketones, Esters, Alcohols, Aromatic Hydrocarbons, Aliphatic Hydrocarbons, Halogenated Solvents		
Propellent		40.00%
Fluorinated Hydrocarbons		
		100.00%

1-lb. net weight   Made in U.S.A.

Tropical rain forests are being cut down and burned.

The destruction of tropical rain forests is also adding to the greenhouse effect. Trees are being cut down and burned. These burning trees send more carbon dioxide into the atmosphere.

27

A scientist with the U.S. Department of Agriculture researches greenhouse gases in Washington, D.C.

Scientists know that carbon dioxide in our atmosphere has been increasing since the late 1800s because of people's activities. If this increase continues, it could raise the average temperature of the Earth.

THE CHANGES GLOBAL WARMING MIGHT CAUSE

Many scientists believe that if we keep sending greenhouse gases into the atmosphere, the worldwide climate will grow warmer and warmer. Summers would be much hotter and drier. Winters would be milder.

Our Earth would not get so hot that nothing could live here. But there would be great changes.

29

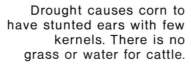
Drought causes corn to
have stunted ears with few
kernels. There is no
grass or water for cattle.

Farming would be the
activity most affected by
worldwide warming. Patterns
of rainfall would change.
The wheat fields and
cornfields of the Midwest
would dry up due to the heat
and lack of rain. Parts of

Canada and Russia that are now too cold for farming would become warmer. These areas would grow most of the world's grain.

While some parts of the world would be drier, other parts would be wetter. Sea levels would rise as the

With global warming, land in northern Canada might grow grain, and ocean shorelines might be underwater.

oceans warm up and as glaciers and polar ice caps begin to melt. This would cause flooding along the coasts of many countries of the world where millions of people live.

There would also be heavy rains and terrible floods in parts of India and Bangladesh.

Floods in Bangladesh (left) turn streets into rivers.
A melting glacier (right) in the Canadian Rockies

STOPPING GREENHOUSE WARMING

The greenhouse warming could be stopped if people stopped adding greenhouse gases to the atmosphere. But this is more difficult than it sounds.

If we stopped all the activities that give off carbon dioxide, our lives would change completely.

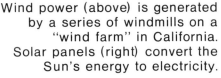
Wind power (above) is generated
by a series of windmills on a
"wind farm" in California.
Solar panels (right) convert the
Sun's energy to electricity.

We could no longer drive
gas-powered cars. We
would have to find other
energy sources. Solar power
or wind power would have to
be used to provide electricity
for our homes, schools, and

offices.

A solar house (left) uses the
Sun's rays for heating.
A solar power plant (below) in France

Scientists say there are
other ways to cut down on
greenhouse gases.
Antipollution devices and
high efficiency car engines
would reduce carbon dioxide.

Old refrigerators and air conditioners containing CFCs could be recycled. Fast-food restaurants could stop packaging hamburgers in plastic foam boxes. Scientists believe we must find and use forms of energy

This abandoned refrigerator (left) contains CFC gases.
Plastic foam food packages also contribute to greenhouse gases.

Atomic power plant (left) in Canada.
A forest (above) in Brazil
that has been destroyed by a
method called slash-and-burn

that do not give off carbon
dioxide. These energy forms
include safer atomic energy
and solar energy.

Stopping the destruction
of the tropical rain forests
would also slow the
greenhouse warming.

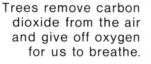
Trees remove carbon
dioxide from the air
and give off oxygen
for us to breathe.

Scientists think we should
plant more trees everywhere
in the world to help use up
the extra carbon dioxide in
the air.

NOT EVERYONE AGREES ON THE GREENHOUSE EFFECT

Many questions about the greenhouse effect remain. No one knows for sure how great a climate change might occur. No one knows exactly when it might happen.

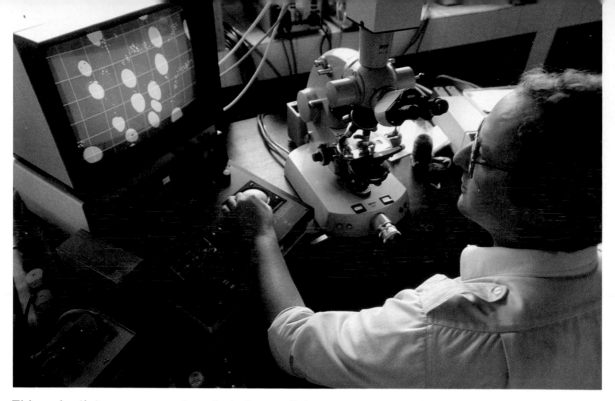

This scientist uses computers to help predict
what changes global warming might cause.

Many scientists say a
global climate change
would cause people great
hardships. They want all the
countries of the world to
start cutting down the
greenhouse gases right now.

Nuclear power plants (left) are very expensive to build and run.
Solar homes (right) are also very costly to build.

But many people disagree.
They say that antipollution
measures are too expensive.
They say that it is too soon to
take such steps, because
no one knows for sure that
a climate change will occur.

To make things even more complicated, other scientists think greenhouse warming may be a good thing. It may put off a new ice age. They have studied Earth's history of cold and warm periods. They say that Earth could be entering another ice age.

During an ice age, glaciers like these cover much of the northern parts of Earth.

FOREST PLANTATION
FIRST HARVEST 1930's
SECOND HARVEST 1984
PLANTED 1986
NEXT HARVEST 2036
JOBS GROW WITH TREES

Foresters plant new trees after clear-cutting,
or removing all the trees from an area.

Who is right? The
scientists who want to take
steps now to avoid global
warming? Or the people
who want to wait and see?

Contour plowing (above) helps conserve
soil. Below: A coral reef in the
South Pacific. Right: Trees preserved
in a national park in Japan.

Antipollution devices that control smoke from factories and gases from car exhausts help reduce greenhouse gases in the atmosphere.

Only time will tell. But the scientists warn that if we wait until we know for sure, it might be too late to prevent the hardships caused by global warming.

WORDS YOU SHOULD KNOW

antipollution (AN • tye • puh • LOO • shun —acting against the dirtying of air or water

atmosphere (AT • muss • fear) —the layer of gases that surrounds Earth and some other planets

carbon dioxide (KAR • bin dye • OX • ide) —a gas made up of carbon and oxygen that is found in the air

CFCs [chlorofluorocarbons] (klor • oh • flur • oh • KAR • bunz) —manufactured gases containing chlorine and fluorine that block the Sun's rays

climate (KLY • mit) —the average kind of weather at a specific place

cycle (SY • kil) —a complete set of events that keeps repeating in the same order

dissolve (dih • ZAHLVE) —to melt in a liquid; to make or become liquid

efficiency (ih • FISH • en • cee) —doing or making something with the least waste of time or materials

gas (GAS) —a substance that is not solid or liquid, but is fluid and able to expand indefinitely

global (GLOH • bil) —covering the whole Earth

grain (GRAYN) —seeds of plants such as wheat and rice, used for food

greenhouse (GREEN • howse) —a building with glass or plastic walls and roof, used for growing plants

hardship (HARD • ship) —difficult living conditions

ice age (ICE AYJ) —a time when the average temperatures are cold and ice sheets cover large parts of Earth

ice cap (ICE KAP) —a covering of ice at the North and South poles of the Earth

methane (METH • ayn) —a colorless, odorless gas that is formed by rotting plants

molecule (MAHL • ih • kyool) —the smallest particle of a substance that can exist and still keep its chemical form

orbiting (OR • bih • ting) — going around something in a regular path

rain forest (RAYN FOR • ist) — a thick forest that grows in the tropics, where there is much rain

ray (RAY) — energy traveling outward from an object such as the Sun

recycle (re • SY • kil) — to use again; to break down into its parts for reuse

rice paddies (RYCE PAD • eez) — fields covered with shallow water where rice plants are grown

solar power (SO • ler POW • er) — energy from the Sun's rays used to do work for people

tropical (TRAH • pih • kil) — growing or living near the equator, an imaginary line around the center of the earth

water vapor (WAW • ter VAY • per) — water that has been heated until it becomes a gas

wind power (WIHND POW • er) — energy from the force of the wind used to do work by people

INDEX

About the Author

Darlene R. Stille is a Chicago-based science writer and editor.

DATE DUE

SEP 15 1991			
NOV 18 1991			
DEC 6 1991			
JAN 9 1992			
JAN 16 1992			
FEB 7 1992			
MAY 21			
APR 23 1993			
OCT			
DEC			
GAYLORD			PRINTED IN U.S.A.